SEA SMOKE TO ASHES

Poems

Carlos Reyes

Cyberwit.net
HIG 45 Kaushambi Kunj, Kalindipuram
Allahabad - 211011 (U.P.) India
http://www.cyberwit.net
Tel: +(91) 9415091004 +(91) (532) 2552257
E-mail: info@cyberwit.net

Printed at Repro India Limited.

To Karen
with me always on my journeys

&

To Mike, Amy, Nina, & Rachel
who bring a special light into my life

ACKNOWLEDGMENTS

The author is particularly indebted to his main supporter and in-house editor, Karen Checkoway.

Special thanks to The Island Institute of Sitka, Alaska for awarding me the residency where some of these poems were written.

... light sifts

through the air like ash.

"Psyche" by Laurie Sheck

Contents

IV
Chekhov's Hammer

V
Like a Moth

I

Awake in the Dark

Just as I Fall Asleep

The voice says *Helen*,
then gone. Only a dial tone,
the message erased leaving
only the caller's name.

On the message pad next to the phone
To: still staring blankly at me.
From: a prairie of white space.
Message: staffs ready for clefs and notes,

only one word superimposed.

But here in the night
her voice leaves me
unsettled, wondering.

Is there some detail
from our last conversation my sister
left out and wants to tell me now?
Her words then were clear and final,

the conflict between us long
since settled as we stand talking

beneath dripping firs
on the banks of the Trask
where her remains are returned.

What's Left of Memory

Your feet still feel
the trail, once
trampled grass
before snow came.

With thawing
grass springs back,
wet sharp blades
between the toes.

Recall can lie:
you never walked that trail
barefoot, it was always
marching boots.

What's left of memory
in the dark footlocker:
stiff soles,
those boots.

Flat Black

Behind me the rumor
of coming winter
from farther up than
the Great Slave Lakes

Fronts girdled somewhere
north of the Arctic Circle

It's August by the calendar

A whisper says
tonight is the last night
the sun sets after 8

From this date
we tremble like paper,
like aspen leaves then fall
onto the floor of shorter days

Less lighted, darkening skies
like unwanted self-knowledge,
a flat black we never painted

our innermost thoughts
our darkest moments

Mad Accordion

Getting lost in a book
is not like getting lost in a storm,
not like getting lost
in the city, not like

getting lost in the fog
even if you think the droplets
condensing are words,
the coming wind will blow away

whole sentences you wipe
from your brow like thoughts
with a handkerchief.
But getting lost without the book

you were reading, the lost book
left dying by the campfire,
the book you threw out
on the curb in the gutter,

after a downpour
exploding into
a mad silent accordion.

Chekhov Before Sleep

In the background
Anton flees, a shadow

crossing a stringless musical instrument.
Beneath it a roach

barely maintains its position,
swims murky water

the way my unhurried thoughts travel
through these clouded nights.

Scythe

If the moon is
a scythe
what does it reap?

No fields of wheat
these waves, these combers.

The rusty bow
of a steel ship

goes aground
again
and again.

My Icelandic Blanket

has lipstick
prints from someone
who once slept here.
The blanket

a gift dear to me
one of the few
possessions
I came away with

after 13 years.
I like to think
the lips permanently
imprinted on the blanket

were my wife's.
I take it from the sea chest
feel its warmth.
No longer

is she in my dreams
of strange nights
in Iceland.

When You Left

Because your side of the bed was abandoned
I stacked all the books in a pile.

They accumulated, took on
your form, were silent as books,

but never turned their backs on me. Because
I imagined them level with me

pointed and hard, pyramids of your breasts—
they were but tents over words,

nothing under them but pages
of dried syllables and consonants.

When I tired of looking at that quiet cordillera
I threw the patchwork coverlet over them.

Because the long quilt-covered mound
looked like a freshly filled grave

I deconstructed you, picked up the books,
closed them, exiled them

to the other sightless room.

The Waking Table

Quito's marble moon
holds containers of ash,
two poets in leather bags

pushed together, end
to end, wrapped in alpaca wool,
a heavy blanket-like shroud.

We don't put them in crypts just
to have them broken out, ashes
thrown up like an eruption

onto the Andean winds, scattered
with Pichincha's cinders.

We leave the iron door ajar,
welcome the jackals to come,
take the remains to a hidden cave.

I say *Adios amigos,*
walk away, try to find
the waking table of poets.

Dictionaries of Paraguay

Two lakes, both private.
I must ask permission to swim there.
A woman, apparently the owner, asks
Who are you? I reply

Soy el gringo blanco de tus sueños.

One lake is brown with turtles and snakes.
I swim in it, see no snakes, only turtle heads.
The other body

of water is crystal
clear, marked out by a boundary
of evenly spaced tiger paws.

We are in South America.

Windsock

The single sleeve
of wind, torn
from the vast blue
shirt.

The pilot in leather
helmet
and goggles
strains.

He doesn't trust
the illusion
he's flying into.

Mobile

Tiny balsa bombers
hang over baby's crib.

Planes twirl in the night hours.

> *Twirling over Budapest*
> *before they return home,*

> *over Berlin where lights below*
> *twinkle, go out*

> *over the crumbled darkness,*
> *phosphorus blossoming*

> *like fields of wild carrots.*

Baby might be sleeping peacefully.
As father sees the lights go out

mother waits for the bombers to stop
twirling in the shadowed room.

> *Waiting for the bombs finned like*
> *fish to stop screaming*

> *as she and the neighbors rush*
> for shelter.

> *She waits for the whistling to die*
> into baby's whispered breath.

II

Ashes

Ashes

Take rusted and bent nails
saved to make a rough box

without a square or tape to measure with.
For sure there's a tree somewhere

beneath the rough surface of scrap lumber.
Shave a bit of old cedar wood

you'll smell its essence.
Taste the rust you'll know iron.

If this were an old cigar box,
its ghost-scent of tobacco and cedar,

you'd say it's a safe place
for ashes of flesh and bones,

but too elegant for this half-assed carpenter,
a man who never smoked cigars.

Omnipresence

As I put my book away
she was at the door
of the empty classroom.
Your father she whistled

through false teeth.
Before I could speak,
gone the whisk of slippers
along a silver corridor.

Years later I wake
to a touch on my shoulder.
I'm here, she whispers
through clattering dentures,

weaving loose fingers
in the receding light.

One Long Sentence

Moorless we drift
through darkness

holding our breath, waiting
for the saving bump

that tells us we have
gone aground on the shore

of some unwelcome
undiscovered island,

creased the perilous reef
just under the surface or

our keel has sliced the dark
rubbery back

of some behemoth rising
suddenly beneath us.

Whale Song

Great grey whale
surfacing. A whole boatload
we could all stand easily
atop your lichen speckled back

singing hope to the blue sky,
beckoning to crowds onshore.
Singing but not too loudly for fear
that in your yearning for the depths

you will dive, leaving us
swimming for land
through dark molasses
swirling torbellinos

of dream kelp.

III

Sea Smoke

The Bell of Ice Rings in His Glass

North: ice cracks
glaciers break into the sea
avoiding passing ships.

On watch
he bats his gloves together
to keep warm and jumps
from foot to foot.

Tears freeze
the corners
of his eyes.

Out there so long
what he's on look-out for
forgotten.

The ice bell
when it rings:
transparent sparks
form bails of aurorae.

He imagines
a scarred mahogany bar in
Ketchikan, ice
rattles in his drink, rattles him.

On an Island, Again

In an archipelago
the islands

are shards
of ice,

suddenly shattered,
leaving slivers

of jagged
translucent glass.

Rough daggers
chipped green obsidian

like all islands pointing

at my heart.

— Baranof Island, Alaska

Song of the Wandering Anglo

We should go naked to an island.

But before we can appreciate
the new land we must leave behind
our baggage.

We come here fully clothed
in our mores, cultures and histories.

We are all from someplace else except the Tlingit
—true, they came here from another world
but they shed their old skins thousands of years ago.

They wonder why we came, how we wandered,
got lost here or ran aground on the rocks.

Spanish, Russian and now us, the Anglos.
The Tlingit ask: Is the wind not cold enough
to drive you back south with the birds in winter?

Still fully clothed, we take this for Eden and stay.

Arriving in Anchorage to Darkness

We drink up the afternoon hours on the flight.
Somewhere between Portland and Anchorage we lose twilight.
We are in Alaska's sudden darkness.

In Quito on the equator it's light / it's dark
a light switch occurrence.

Eight degrees north of the line in Panama
between day and night, light
melts away like ice in our drinks.

Ketchikan Nights, and Days

Time to dance with women of sandpaper
hands, women who work in the cannery.

Time to have a few in the notorious Fo'c'sle,
risk a fight, chance getting thrown in jail.

Time to walk to the bridge over Ketchikan Creek.
If you catch high tide you can watch salmon

by the hundreds fight their way upstream,
all those fish heading home. But

if upstream is home, it's the funeral home.
Birth, death, food for the young.

Time to stand and think
about the cycle. *Time*

to listen to flowing water.

Carbon Footprint

The Russians logged this slope,
the skirt of Mt. Verstovia, made charcoal

to heat their Samovars.
Later they handed over

their residue—vast domains
they didn't own—to Americans from the south.

Hiking the trail today
my boot kicks up a square of charcoal.

It is miniscule as historical detritus goes.
Hemlock, spruce and cedar

grown up around the pit, the muskeg
almost buries it, as the Russians buried their dead

in the shipwreck cemetery, left St Michaels
and a building or two. But here

in New Archangel there are no descendants.

Shipwreck Cemetery

Do not build houses on sand,
the bible warns us.

We could add: never
build on muskeg, never bury the dead there.

We bury the body on a hill,
nearest to heaven. But what if

the hill is muskeg and rolls
with each frost and thaw like a ship rocking.

We walk through the rusting gate
of the Russian Cemetery on Observatory Hill

face warnings of penalties for vandalizing
tombs. But nobody warned mother nature:

crypts slide down the hill
like sledges. A vault enclosure

looks like and old bed frame
tossed out onto the heap.

Crosses broken, tilted; one wooden head
stone split, another with a heart cut out

to allow a view: a garden
of broken gravestones. Fingers

of spruce join in on this mayhem.
finish the job, break up everything,

here in Death's shipwreck.

New Archangel

"There are no Russians here."

In the Russian American Trading Company
the shopkeeper says they didn't colonize, stayed on the coast.

They came, conquered the Tlingits — they thought —
traded seal skins for ships, sailed home.

There are no Russians here, the Russian shopkeeper
repeats, finishes his day, fills the shelves

with decorated lacquered boxes
and nests of dolls, all made of birch from the taiga.

Sea Smoke

Grandfathers: famous
sailing troll fishermen
of Bristol Bay

Brothers: working
big steel boats,
crabbers, draggers

At the edge
of the great Bering Sea
the bells of St George toll

beneath onion domes and
log cabin churches.
Missionaries brought

baptism, bibles
orthodoxy to The Pribilofs
these small rocks

Great-grandfather: in his *bidarka*
through waves and ice floes
hunted grey whale and fur seal

The belles of St George
come now to Anchorage
to halibut canneries

and bars where we talk
in the long night
I dance and dance

to rock and roll
with a belle
of St George

Wake instead with
a smoky memory salt
chapped hands in mine

Through the sea smoke
she says: *All I want
is to return to St George*

*all I need
is enough
to get back*

*climb to
the top of Ulakaia
look out to sea*

*Anchorage hundreds
of miles away
a memory*

*walk the beaches
Walrus Island
with Uncle George*

search the depths
of bones for the prize
an ivory tusk

hear the bells
of St George
calling

Mass sung
the priest
more Aleut than Russian

whose name
is the same as mine
instead of dancing

here with you.

Jailed Poet Leaves Soviet Ivory Tower

— for Irina Ratushinskaya

As I dry my hands
I see on the shelf
the cake of soap: Ashes

of Roses.
I think of you
in the cell,
washing your hands

with those poems
after committing them
to memory. Your
fingers thin

as matchsticks,
instruments
of your creations;
burned out matches

transfer the fire
of your work
to the bar of soap.
Surely, of the hundreds

you carved,
one was misplaced:

Ashes of Roses,
swirling down the drain,

into Siberian rivers
to the Bering Sea.

12/18/86

IV

Chekhov's Hammer

Aura

Hotter than the hinges of hell, they say.
But I say those glowing hinges
support a door I can't open.

I watch as flames begin —
the door glows solid.

Through the inverted aura
of the door is a room
of dancing women, and men
adoring the women dancing.

But the dancing is frenetic
veils cover glowing visages
men's faces burn in adoration
all the way to ash.

Faithless Love

The spider web gown billows
in a whisper, then trails
in the dew as she steps
through the forest

to a wedding. She doesn't know
how it came from the hem
to wrap itself around her blood
suffused neck. The spider web

that they press into the wounds
staunch the flow
but those are
ancient times. She could

believe in those black
silken threads, the cross
hairs in the scope of a sniper's
rifle as she sights

down the long tunnel
at the silhouette, her
not quite forgotten
faithless love.

Reel to Reel

The reels of our lives
are unwound, tangled,
sun faded.

We might restore those tapes
if we knew how,
edit our lives.

We have more
than one, don't we?

But I don't
want to walk that dim hallway

to choose, call me
pessimistic.

Burn those reels,
make a great fire.
Sift the ashes,

spread them across
the glass table separating us.

Tell my fortune.

Chekhov's Hammer

Behind the door
of every heart

stands someone
with a hammer

beating out the rhythm
on an anvil

reminding us only
that the spring of blood

keeps flowing
into the rivers of the body

— at times silently
at other times with music

whether the heart
is happy or not

Woman in the Elevator

I'm trapped in the back of the elevator.
She kisses me on the cheek.
Someone very familiar
kisses me sweetly a promise.

She smiles she waves is gone
before I can unsqueeze myself
on the first floor *Wait* I try
only bubbles slip out

floating soap bubbles
hovering momentarily over my head
bubbles filled with upside down
question marks in bubbles

soon lost in the clouds
as my eyes open to morning sun
light through rain washed glass
out the modern enclosed elevator

running up the building.
I glimpse the balloon
the last bubble drifting upward
To the east no question marks

but my dull red lead heart
ripped still pumping from my chest
jagged shreds of my superior
vena cava, red ribbons trailing out.

Distant but still visible by now
my heart a tiny fist barely
recognizable before it falls from
the bubble that bursts on the point

of a 300-year-old Sitka spruce.
I want out, now!
But it's jam packed I can't
get out I see her coming

this way her forefinger nail
as red as my heart used to be
is pointed gun-like at me
or ready to push the button,

any button but her hot pink
lips form around *I'm sorry*
about your heart...
All this is in a bubble

coming from *her* mouth
a bubble full of exclamations
semi-colons unconvincing
double — quick — double — dashes.

Affaire d'Coeure

Flecks of ashes
of wooden tears
or the ash

that fell from
the last bedroom
cigarette

Black chalk
dust of love's bones
cremated

in the last flame

Lament

— for Derek Walcott

The song in the flue of the fireplace, what
does it take from the room besides air

if smoke is fire's guilt? And if
a sudden downdraft brings smoke

back into the room? The gods
have rejected our pitiful sins.

The skirling voice of the confessor:
is this all you bring me?

Truth seeps through a pin hole
in a leaded glass window

of veracity's abandoned home.

Lyric

I wake to the
taste of burnt honey,
caress of warming sunrise.
Through an open window

call of birds,
the day pulling me from ashes
of roses covering
startled breasts, sweet

breath of every spring.

V

Like a Moth

The Wisdom of Crows

They come for lunch in the yard,
at twilight convene in the huge limbs
of the American walnut,
anxious for their moon.

But for now they wait for the cold
wind that sends us into a shiver
when they will frolic
into the forlorn fierce east gale.

The wisdom of their blackness
escapes us, a cautionary tale.
Yet we wait eager

to take on their trappings, to be one
with the crows, to make them
our earnest correspondents.

Alarm

wakes him, he gropes for
glasses to see time,

staggers down
steep worn stairs.

In the kitchen he
finds the teakettle,

goes to the rush
of fresh water from the spigot,

plugs the kettle in
to the next big river.

He waits for water to boil
for day to begin.

While he slept
the tea bag in his cup

like a paper moth
flew from Ireland.

Inversion

Because you worried all night
fell asleep as the sun came up.

Because morning clouds crept in
to cover everything,

darkness covers you.
Because you flew

through the deck of cards
found no aces, no bullets.

Because morning clouds left
only the skeletal bridge.

Letting Go

Every screaming nail
holds boards together

screeches like fingers
on a blackboard.

They want to hold on
like we do.

But it's wind screaming
though a whorl.

It's wind people
screaming for mercy, pleading

Let go.

The 71

As I walk the pre-dawn
the 71 passes each day
on its regular schedule
whether I'm here or not,

its passengers hardly awake
on their way to jobs they hate,
traveling to the last day
of school, going home

to sleep after unremitting night.
One found a ticket in the trash
rides free: he hates waste.

He understands the numbers on the paper
slip: knows the code, has one hour left
on his journey. Passengers all, no one
travels with such certainty.

The Milk Run

In Greenwich Village
we talk of those who died,
those dying, loves gone
wrong. Past midnight

at Grand Central
we board the train north
and fall into sleep
to the litany

of every small station
after Harlem:
nodding off
into Bronxville.

The milk run, our only choice,
the last train, awake
now at our own stop.

We walk away from the train,
its cars empty
heading for the final station.

Abandonment

Out in a field of stubble
in the night the train stops
its one headlight still searching
for the rails it lost.

The engineer abandons
his locomotive, goes off
with the switchman's lantern
looking for the next station,

sees nothing behind but two tracks
in the mud, nothing ahead
but dark skies and sprinkles
of stars. As they abandon

the stalled train, passengers
wipe stars like sleep from their eyes.

Captive

Time is wire-
brushed away

from the rusty metal,
mushroomed

stake driven
deep into dark loam.

When rust returns
tomorrow

who will scrub it, who
then will dream time,

rope holding the animal
frayed into wind?

Transient

Sleeping highway
billboards

drooping eyelids,
headlights

The long wet tread
of slick tires

print our passing.

www.ingramcontent.com/pod-product-compliance
Lightning Source LLC
LaVergne TN
LVHW041116180726
843490LV00003B/1030